Guided Meditation for Building Happiness

Use The Law of Attraction with Meditation, Hypnosis and Positive Affirmations for Manifesting Prosperity, Success, Self-Love and Weight Loss

Olivia Clifford

"Guided Meditation for Building Happiness: Use The Law of Attraction with Meditation, Hypnosis and Positive Affirmations for Manifesting Prosperity, Success, Self-Love and Weight Loss." Written by "Olivia Clifford".

Guided Meditation for Building Happiness is a set of the books "Guided Meditation for The Law of Attraction" & "Master Meditation and The Law of Attraction".

Hope You Enjoy!

© **Copyright 2021 - All rights reserved.**

The content contained within this book may not be reproduced, duplicated or transmitted without direct written permission from the author or the publisher.

Under no circumstances will any blame or legal responsibility be held against the publisher, or author, for any damages, reparation, or monetary loss due to the information contained within this book, either directly or indirectly.

Legal Notice:

This book is copyright protected. It is only for personal use. You cannot amend, distribute, sell, use, quote or paraphrase any part, or the content within this book, without the consent of the author or publisher.

Disclaimer Notice:

Please note the information contained within this document is for educational and entertainment purposes only. All effort has been executed to present accurate, up to date, reliable, complete information. No warranties of any kind are declared or implied. Readers acknowledge that the author is not engaged in the rendering of legal, financial, medical or professional advice. The content within this book has been derived from various sources. Please consult a licensed professional before attempting any techniques outlined in this book.

Table of Contents

Guided Meditation for The Law of Attraction

Introduction

Chapter One: The Law of Attraction

Chapter Two: Guided Meditation

Chapter Three: Hypnosis

Chapter Four: Self-hypnosis Scripts

Chapter Five: Powerful Affirmations for Self-Improvement

Conclusion

Master Meditation and The Law of Attraction

Introduction

Chapter 1: The Law of Attraction

Mindfulness

Chapter 2: Meditation and Hypnosis

Chapter 3: Affirmations

Chapter 4: Breathing

Chapter 5: Guided Meditation for the Law of Attraction

Chapter 6: Guided Hypnosis for the Law of Attraction

Conclusion

References

Guided Meditation for The Law of Attraction

Powerful Affirmations, Guided Meditation, and Hypnosis for Love, Money, Weight Loss, Relationships, and Happiness!

Olivia Clifford

Introduction

Sometimes it can be so difficult to change your unwanted behaviors, attitudes, or situations. Have you ever wondered why? For instance, why can't addicted smokers just make one emphatic decision to stop smoking? Why can't you just decide once to stop anxiety and just relax more and enjoy life? Here is a quick revelation. Your mind has it all. One part of you agrees to change. And another part says "no way". It is like each of us has two minds which disagree on what should and shouldn't change.

Your mind is a very complex entity, and it is difficult to totally understand it. But, know that each of us has one mind with two different aspects — conscious and subconscious. Your conscious mind includes your current awareness. It is part of you that decides on what to do or where to go. Your subconscious is the part of your mind that works below the surface of your awareness. It has access to all your memories, holds your beliefs and values, and efficiently recalls all your frequently used behavior patterns. Your subconscious mind also runs the body functions like breathing, digestion, and many other tasks which you've never thought of.

Your subconscious and conscious mind work together. However, the subconscious mind is resistant to the sudden change that's why sometimes it appears to be working against the conscious mind. This is mainly because of "programming," especially when you attempt to change a longstanding habit, behavior, belief, or attitude.

Your mind is like a computer. Just like a computer has installed programs, so does your mind. Your behavioral sequence and thought patterns are examples of such 'programs'. You and others by other people (parents, teachers, peers, etc install some of these 'programs'.). We have a saying in computer programming— "Garbage in, garbage out." It simply means, if you input the wrong data in the computer, you will get the wrong output. Therefore, what you put in your mind is what you get or experience. If you feed your mind with negative thoughts and vibes, you get failure as an output.

Just like computer programs need to be activated with the right commands, so do your mind programs. Whenever a certain sequence of thoughts, words, or events occurs, your mind programs are ready and waiting in the subconscious mind to be activated. This usually works to your advantage, as it is the very essence of learning. However, sometimes you may realize that you input some garbage (negative thoughts and vibes) in your mind long ago and you no longer need them; you want to get rid of them. Perhaps you simply want to reprogram your mind by adding a new attitude, or behavior, that appeals to you.

Changing your subconscious mind's programs is not a simple thing. However, if you reprogram your subconscious mind, you can completely change your life. Your mind comes with a filter, a protector that acts as an inbuilt security system. This filter screens new thoughts, beliefs, and behaviors, ensuring that you want what you say you want. It is very slow for accepting sudden changes that are inconsistent with your old thoughts, behaviors, or beliefs.

Your subconscious mind is nondiscriminatory; this works to your benefit to keep your beliefs, behaviors, and personality consistent. Here, any idea or suggestion that is allowed past the mental filter is accepted as true. To avoid ending up in a state of confusion, the security system prevents you from changing your mind and accepting every suggestion that comes your way. However, this can be troublesome if you want to change something in your life for your good. The mind's security system can always reject ideas and even suggestions from your conscious thoughts. It can prevent you from reprogramming your mind with good ideas and positive vibes for change. It does this because it evaluates the new ideas, even good ones based on the previously accepted beliefs and interpretation of experience.

We have several ways to deal with the security system of your subconscious mind to enable change in your life. But, some ways are more expedient than others. Some people, for instance, repeat a new behavior until it becomes a habit. This method has its challenges but some iron-willed souls who persevere sometimes change themselves, because repeating an activity several times can override the subconscious mind's security system. Your inner mind eventually accepts the fresh ways of doing things and becomes a habit.

This book offers you powerful and preferable tools for change. It discusses the most expedient methods of reprogramming your mind. If you want to stay happy, lose weight, attract money, love and relationships, this book is for you. If you believe, it is going to help you rid yourself of all the negativity that has been holding you back. It starts by discussing the law of attraction, then it goes further and provides guided meditation exercises, affirmations, and self-hypnosis scripts for self-improvement. You only need to be committed to performing the exercises and you will never regret a single second spent on this book. Life is too short to spend it broken, miserable, and depressed. Here is the change you want and a solution to all your problems!

Chapter One: The Law of Attraction

Do you ever feel that sometimes things happen exactly how you want them to? The things that you need just fall into place or come to you from out-of-the-blues? Have you ever bumped into someone you were thinking about on the streets? Or a chance phone call from a lost friend just as you needed their help over something? Perhaps you've met your life partner or gotten your dream job just by fate or virtue of being at the right place at the right time. If you've ever experienced any of these, then you were experiencing the law of attraction. Some people find themselves in inappropriate relationships repeatedly. Perhaps your friend or relative has complained to you that they keep attracting the same kind (bad) of relationships. The law of attraction is at work for them as well. There is a fundamental force in the universe that guides people's lives and it is the underlying power behind all things—the law of attraction.

What Exactly is the Law of Attraction?

The law of attraction according to Napoleon Hill states that "we attract into our lives whatever we focus on". Put in simple terms, you get whatever you give your energy and attention to, be it positive or negative. The definition is simple but has a lot of meaning and truth in it. You are the one who creates your experiences, the surrounding people, the things that you receive, and your universe. You create them with the power of your thoughts.

This truth has spread to many people and has more recently been expressed in a popular quote:

Be careful with your thoughts, for they translate into words.

Be careful with your words, for they translate into actions.

Be careful of your actions, for they become habits.

Be careful of your habits, for they become character.

Be careful of your character, for it becomes your destiny.

The law of attraction tells us that whatever we give our attention to becomes what we magnetize into our lives.

How Does the Law of Attraction Work?

The basic premise of the law of attraction is "like attracts like". This means that two entities vibrating at the same frequencies pull towards each other. You can attract good things in your life when you have positive thoughts. The reverse is also true. Negative thoughts can bring you things that you don't want. You send out positive energy when you feel happy or loved. You send out negative energy when you feel bored, anxious, or stressed out.

Through the law of attraction, the universe responds enthusiastically to both vibrations. Based on the type of energy you create, it gives you more of it. It doesn't choose for you the best. Your energy vibrations attract the same frequencies back to you. Therefore, whatever you feel or think is your request to the universe for more of the same. Being aware of your energy, feelings, and thoughts are therefore very important. It helps you send out vibrations that resonate with what you want.

7 Steps for Deliberate Attraction

Know what you desire

Knowing exactly what you desire is key to attracting what you want. This gives the universe a simple time to act upon your desires. Most still don't know exactly what they truly want in life. The best way to desire something is to be specific.

You might say 'I would like more money, a good job, a good husband' however that's not enough. You must specify what you want.

'I would like a tall, handsome, stable, hardworking, loving, and respectful husband. I see myself walking with him along the beach and making love to each other'. Now, that is the proper way to know what you exactly want.

Be specific in your desires and visualize your emotions in your mind. The vibrations of your emotions are the ones that will make the law of attraction come alive.

Give your desire attention and ask the universe for it

The law of attraction gives you more of what you pay your attention to, put your energy and focus on. Meditate, and when you are calm, ask the universe for what you truly want. We are born in a universe where there are enough resources for everyone. The world "owes you a living". Your genuine desires are your "birth rights". But you have to know how to claim it.

Believe that they will come

The actual key to manifesting your desires is belief. It is very simple, it will not work for you if you don't believe it. You may say that I can't believe in something you cannot see. We have a solution for that: start small and remove any doubt. Act as if you already have it. Take moments out of your day-to-day life and re-experience what the sights and feelings are after you have been granted your desire. Just experience it as vividly as possible. The outcome will amaze you.

Use guided meditation to manifest your desires

Visualizing your desires in exact details can do wonders to your powers of manifestation. Your desires are brought to you a lot quicker if you visualize or use guided meditation to manifest them. Guided meditation is one of the best ways to infuse your mind. You take on a journey in your mind and help you to manifest the specific desire in your life. If you want something to happen in your life, think about it first. For instance, if you want an excellent partner, picture him/her in your mind, picture yourself enjoying life with the partner. You will see him/her and at long last, you have that life partner you wanted.

Inner dialogue

Be conscious of your inner dialogue and change the way you talk to yourself. Whatever you utter comes to pass. Your subconscious mind gets to work automatically and helps you make your desires real when you infuse your thoughts with what you desire in life. Using positive affirmations is one of the best ways to introduce new thoughts into your mind. If you practice positive thinking every day, your energy changes and attracts positive things in your life.

Allow it and Let go

Allowing is simply the absence of negative vibration, and any form of doubt is a negative vibration. You know you are allowing your desire when you hear yourself saying statements such as "Ah, what a relief!", "You know, maybe I can have this", or "Now this feels possible." Once you've set your desire in motion and allowed it, it is important to let go of your desire. Don't hold on to it too tight. Holding on to your desire too tight can kill it; it is like a butterfly. Hold on to it lightly and be free to enjoy life forever.

Thank the universe for granting your desire

Gratitude is very important in everything in life. Be grateful for everything you receive in life. Thank the universe for granting your desires. You infuse your thoughts and feelings with positive vibration energy when you practice gratitude in your daily life. This helps you to manifest more of your desires in life. The gratitude should come from your heart. Do it with passion, love, and positivity. Don't just do it in a rote fashion.

Now that you have learned about what the law of attraction is, how it works, and the steps involved in deliberate attraction, you now get more of what you want and less of what you don't want. This is not the end, we are going to learn more in the later chapters. The next chapter expounds more on guided meditation and provides you with exercises to help you attract money, love, relationships, happiness, and lose weight ASAP!

Chapter Two: Guided Meditation

Life treats us differently, but we all lead a hectic one. Nowadays, stress has become an inalienable part of our lives. Good enough, there are ways to control and prevent stress from getting to you. Meditation can help you with this. Meditation is the best way to order your life. Guided meditation is an effective paradigm that fits in with today's busy lifestyle. Using guided meditation techniques to reveal your life purpose is a deeply profound experience. It improves your creativity, health, wealth, and general quality of your life a thousand-fold.

Whether you have been practicing the law of attraction exercises for some time now or you are a novice, you probably know that meditation is an extremely powerful tool. You will hear people who have made it in life talk about the role of guided meditation. However, many manifestation books are shallow and skim over the details of this technique. They also cannot show you how to do it for specific goals.

In this chapter, we aim to tell you all you need to know. We will start by taking you through the benefits of guided meditation and the tips for successful manifestation meditation. Finally, we will show you how to perform specific guided meditation that attracts general good, love, money, relationships, happiness, and weight loss. If you are ready to attract all these, let's dive in!

Benefits of Guided Meditation

There are many benefits gained through meditation. Some of these benefits include stress relief, creativity stimulation, pain relief, sleep improvement, and positive influence on the state of mind. In this section, however, we are going to look at how meditation helps manifest and helps you to attract more positive vibes. Below are some ways you can use guided meditation for manifesting:

It helps you identify and overcome some of your manifestation blocks

For you to achieve your goals and be successful in life, know and overcome the blocks that are holding you back. Guided meditation is one of the most helpful tools in overcoming these manifestation blocks. Meditation helps you forget the outside world and completely switch off to listen to yourself.. You remove most of your abundance blocks. Guided meditations help you change your mindset and beliefs, thus steering your emotions and feelings in a more positive direction.

Guided meditation keeps you more aligned with the universe

Distraction and negative beliefs are the greatest enemies to a successful manifestation. Guided meditation helps you remove the distractions of the outside world and get into a flow state. Success in the law of attraction requires you to fully concentrate and focus on your goal. Guided meditations help you do just that.

Guided meditation trains your intuition and helps you take action

The law of attraction works only if you take action; it is not a magic formula. Through guided meditation, you can strengthen your intuition and attract creative ideas.

Guided meditation can help you become positive and attract more positive vibes

One rule of the law of attraction is "like attracts like". You need a positive attitude to manifest your dream life successfully. Try as much as possible to distance yourself from negative feelings and thoughts. Guided meditation can help you with that.

Guided meditation can help you visualize your dream life

One of the most powerful tools for the law of attraction is visualization; it helps you manifest faster and better. Sometimes you may struggle with visualizing your dreams and goals. In most cases, distractions will cause this. Guided meditation can be of great help here.

Tips for Successful Guided Meditation

Find a peaceful spot

Find a place that is comfortable and quiet; free from external distractions. While meditating, it is natural to find your mind wandering, especially for beginners. Noise and other forms of distraction can make it difficult for you to concentrate and center yourself. Your seating arrangement is also very important. Experiment with original positions to discover what relaxes you. Choose a seating position that calms you down and makes you comfortable.

Posture

Sitting cross-legged with your hands placed on your lap is the ideal posture for meditating. However, earlier, choose what is comfortable for you. Don't force yourself if it is not working for you. Choose a posture that you can manage in the beginning.

Focus

Narrow your focus by concentrating on your breathing. Breathing helps you calm down and prepare you for the actual meditation process. Master the technique of deep breathing and do it well. Notice how your chest rises and falls when breathing in and out, respectively. When distracted, don't judge yourself but gently return your attention to your breathing.

Visualize your desires

Picture what you want to attract using the full force of your imagination. Build this image using all senses. For example, if you're working to manifest money, how will it feel to hold in your arms? What will it smell like? What texture does the money have? Spend as much time building and inhabiting this image as you want.

Embrace your Gratitude

Picture the things that you already have and tune into a deep feeling of gratitude. This helps you attract more abundance into your life.

Finish with tranquility

Pay attention to your surroundings once you are ready to end the session. Notice the movements and the surrounding sounds. Sift your attention to your body to allow the integration to occur. Slowly open your eyes.

Guided Meditation Exercises

You now understand how guided meditation can be a shortcut to boosting your vibes and achieving your goals. You also know how to have a successful meditation session. Let's put it into practice.

Try as much as you can to set aside 15 minutes every day to perform these exercises.

Guided Meditation Exercise to attract Good

Find a comfortable and quiet place and sit comfortably. With your body relaxed and eyes closed, take a few slow, deep inhalations and exhalations.

Bring any recurring patterns to your awareness and take a few moments to observe the patterns and your reaction to them.

Start noticing the negative thoughts or beliefs that perpetuate the recurring patterns.

Next, ask your higher self to help you identify things that are contributing to your current situation.

Begin by bringing one major theme to your mind. Think of all the different moments in your life that this pattern has been present. Notice what happened to you during that time and where you were.

During that period, what was your mindset? What emotions and feelings did you experience?

How did you express yourself? What was your reaction to what was happening? Did something bring this pattern to an end?

What key takeaway do you have from this experience and your reactions to it? What lesson did you learn from the past that can help you activate the law of attraction to attract positive experiences in the future?

Now, let go of what is not helping you to clear out old wounds and beliefs from the past.

Imagine that you're bringing down healing from God, spirit, or the universe to heal you from inside and fill you with new positive energy.

Once you are filled with this healing energy, start visualizing the person, belief, or pattern that you want to dissolve. Imagine flowing this healing from your heart to your external being and ask it to be healed as well.

Say what is needed to say to bring this energy down. Ask your higher self to guide you and then imagine breaking the energetic cord that connects you to this situation and see it dissolved completely.

Now, manifest what you wanted to. Visualize it in the brightest, colorful, exciting, and joy-filled way. Act as if you already have it. Notice how happy you are and feel the positive emotions running through you. Be grateful for all the gifts this life has given upon you.

When you feel that what you're seeing is powerful and real, inhale deeply. As you breathe out, imagine energizing everything you have with this visual representation.

While still sitting, notice the internal shifts allowing the integration to occur. Slowly open your eyes when you are ready.

Guided Meditation Exercise for Happiness

Sit or lie down comfortably in a quiet place. Take a deep breath in and close your eyes as you exhale.

Take a moment and recall the intention for today's practice: to welcome happiness as your birthright.

Notice any negative thoughts and limiting beliefs that act against your happiness and release them to free yourself.

Take a moment and recall your heartfelt desire—happiness

Ask your higher self to guide you. Now manifest happiness. Visualize it in a joy-filled way.

Notice how happy you are, take in any important sounds, feel the positive vibrations running through you, and steep yourself in gratitude for the gift given to you.

Imagine yourself going about your day, welcoming in joy throughout.

When you feel this image is powerful and real, open and close your eyes several times whilst welcoming in joy.

Sit for a few more moments to notice the internal shifts allowing the integration to occur. Welcome yourself back to your open eyes and alert state of waking consciousness.

Guided Meditation Exercise for Money

Sit comfortably, close your eyes and take a deep breath in and out.

Open your heart and let go of any negative thoughts, beliefs, or anxiety.

Imagine yourself holding huge bundles of money.

Visualize yourself feeling the texture of the notes in your hands, rub them between your fingers, and imagine smelling them.

Imagine yourself matching your bank with your ATM card to withdraw a tremendous amount of money.

Picture yourself withdrawing the money. Imagine you've spent some of the money and are still comfortably well off. Give thanks and open your eyes slowly.

Guided Meditation Exercise for Love & Relationships

Sit or lie down comfortably in a quiet place. Take a deep breath in and close your eyes as you exhale.

Take a moment and recall the intention for today's practice: to find love as your birthright.

Notice any negative thoughts, limiting beliefs, or experiences that prevent you from falling in love. Release them to free yourself.

Take a moment and recall your heartfelt desire—to find the love of your life

Ask your higher self to guide you. Now manifest about them. Imagine how it would be to share your life with them.

Allow that feeling of calmness and completeness to fill you up.

Reflect on what it is to have everything that you need. Notice how happy you are, feel the positive energy running through you, and steep yourself in gratitude.

Imagine the light-emitting magnetic pull attracting others towards you.

When you feel this image is powerful and real. Take a deep breath in and out.

Sit for a few more moments to notice the internal shifts allowing the integration to occur. Welcome yourself back to your open eyes and alert state of waking consciousness.

Guided Meditation Exercise for Weight Loss

Sit or lie down comfortably in a quiet place. Take a deep breath in and close your eyes as you exhale.

Take a moment and recall the intention for today's practice: to become fat-free and fit.

Notice any negative thoughts or limiting beliefs that prevent you from losing weight. Release them to free yourself.

Take a moment and recall your heartfelt desire—to lose weight

Ask your higher self to guide you. Now it is about losing weight. Visualize yourself as beautiful and thinner.

Notice how fit, happy, and confident you are. Feel the positive energy running through you and steep yourself in gratitude.

Imagine yourself strutting around with confidence in those skinny dresses and trousers.

When you feel this image is powerful and real, take a deep breath in and out.

Sit for a few more moments to notice the internal shifts allowing the integration to occur. Welcome yourself back to your open eyes and alert state of waking consciousness.

Key Takeaways

- Early mornings are the best time for meditation
- Choose a peaceful place that is free from noise and distractions
- Your posture is crucial for a successful meditation session
- Focus is equally important. Count while breathing in and out if you find it difficult to focus on your breathing.
- Don't blame yourself or get upset when your mind drifts when meditating
- Always visualize your desires as you meditate
- Always embrace gratitude
- Ensure that you are filled with enthusiasm before starting your meditation journey

Chapter Three: Hypnosis

You must have heard of the term hypnosis. And, if you are like many other people, you must have heard of its effectiveness in helping people achieve their goals. You might even have thought of how you can use hypnosis to change your life. Maybe you would like to be hypnotized to improve your physical body to get lean and trim, find love and better relationships, get more money or stop smoking once and for all. Or, maybe you are stressed in your life and want to be hypnotized to release the tension and feel more relaxed. Who doesn't want to be happy? Who doesn't need love, good health, and wealth? Perhaps you've wondered if hypnosis could help with this. Yes, it can!

Hypnosis: A Recognized Form of Therapy

Hypnosis has been around since time immemorial. This phenomenon has been used as therapy. It was not until the 19th century that a man named Dr. James Braid coined it. Since then, the field of clinical hypnotherapy has been developing. The American Medical Association for inclusion in medical schools even approved hypnosis instruction in the late 1950s. Clinicians have then considered hypnosis a serious topic in the healing arts. Hypnosis is a safe and efficient tool for growth and self-improvement. It does not mean hypnosis for specific people, nearly everyone can be hypnotized. It is easy to learn and use. It doesn't require any fancy equipment to apply it. Once you understand the basic tenets and techniques, self-hypnosis can easily be applied; it is self-therapy that is free of cost. And unlike drug therapies, self-hypnosis does not have negative side effects. It is safe and friendly.

So, what is Hypnosis?

If you ask ten hypnotherapists for the definition of hypnosis, you will get over ten different answers. There is no consensus about the definition of hypnosis. Most of the definitions provided describe how hypnosis is induced rather than what it is. For the sake of instruction, here is a short but broad definition: Hypnosis is a state of narrowed focus in which suggestibility is greatly heightened.

While in this state, positive ideas, values, and images may be impressed upon your subconscious mind to elicit beneficial changes.

Tips for Using Hypnosis for Goal Achievement

1. **Visualize.** Program your subconscious mind with your desired outcome. During self-hypnosis, visually imagine that you have already accomplished your goal and reached your aim. See it as real and experience all the wonderful feelings associated with the attainment of that goal.

2. **Persistence**. Program your subconscious mind to change your inner character traits and have the traits of the people who never give up. Be persistent regardless of your current situation.

3. **Think Positive.** Program your subconscious mind to think positively and expect positive results. Your inner mind tends to replay the memories and throw them into consciousness as doubts and fears. You can eliminate this during self-hypnosis.

4. **Program out the Problem**. When trying to pursue worthwhile goals, inevitably, some problems will arise. You can solve these problems fairly rapidly through self-hypnosis. Just see yourself successfully traversing the obstacle while in a trance.

5. **Pre-pave your path.** Imagine yourself being in the right place at the right time, meeting the right people. Use the power of hypnosis to program your mind like this. Your subconscious mind will pick up on non-verbal clues, process the millions of bits of information you receive every second, and guide you to the right course of action.

6. **Develop faith.** Convince your subconscious mind that your goal is already a reality. "Fake it till you make it". Use self-hypnosis to fool your subconscious mind into believing the "real" world is exactly like the world you have been visualizing.

Step by Step Guide for Self-hypnosis

1. **Make yourself comfortable:** Find a quiet and comfortable place to sit or lie. Have an open posture that is easy to maintain for at least 20 minutes. Take a few slow, deep breaths, allow your eyes to close naturally, and let your mind relax.

2. **Release any tension**: Release any physical tension throughout your body. Imagine each muscle is completely relaxing right from your toes, up to your legs, and on your back. Your shoulders and upper back hold a lot of tension, so spend extra time on them. Visualize your body gradually filling up with a calm, glowing light.

3. **Connect with your subconscious**: To successfully connect with your subconscious mind, roll your eyes back in your head gently and visualize yourself at the top of a staircase. You can imagine anything that can represent your consciousness. It doesn't have to be a staircase. Move your focus from your conscious mind at the top of the staircase to your subconscious at the bottom.

4. **Descend down the stairs slowly, taking one stair at a time**: With each stair take a slow, deep breath and let yourself feel even more relaxed than you did on the previous step, drifting deeper and deeper into your relaxing trance state. Start counting from 10 with each step going down until you get to 1 at the bottom of the staircase.

5. **Place your suggestions into your subconscious:** Once you reach the bottom of the staircase, start implanting hypnotic suggestions that resonate with your desired goal into your subconscious. You can gently repeat one or more of the following phrases in your mind:

    - "I am calm and relaxed"
    - "I do not fear anything"
    - "I am strong and confident"
    - "I now stop this bad habit"
    - "I am in control of my destiny"
    - "I deserve love"
    - "I can have everything I want"
    - "I deserve to have happiness in all areas of my life"
    - "I am healthy and energetic"
    - "I lose body fat safely and easily"
    - "I can remember my dreams"
    - "I feel safe becoming leaner"
    - "I am a lucid dreamer"
    - "I have a powerful drive and motivation to increase my monetary income"
    - Just remember to make every phrase positive and in the present tense.

6. **Wake Up Gently:** Repeat your chosen phrases as many times as you want. Enjoy the feeling of deep relaxation. Prepare to wake up from your trance state when you're ready. Tell yourself that you are going to count up to 10 as you climb up the stairs and with each step, you will slowly return to full awareness. Now start counting from 1 as you climb back up the steps in your mind. When you reach 10, take a deep breath

and then open your eyes. Sit for a moment, then stand up slowly.

Chapter Four: Self-hypnosis Scripts

Before you recite any of these scripts, do the following to induct self-hypnosis environment:

- Find a quiet and comfortable place to sit or lie in an open posture that is easy to maintain for at least 20 minutes. Take a few slow, deep breaths, allow your eyes to close naturally, and let your mind relax.
- Tell yourself that you intend to make this a deep relaxation session.
- Take three deep breaths. Hold your breath for a couple of seconds after breathing in deeply before breathing out
- As you breathe in, imagine that you are taking in all the positive energy that the universe offers as calm, glowing light – feel this light filling up your body and helping you to relax.
- As you breathe out, imagine that the light is moving out of your body into the universe, taking with it all your stress, tension, worries, irritation, and anxieties.
- Starting from your toes, relax your body to your head. Tell that part of your body to relax. Don't force yourself to relax, just allow it to happen all by itself.
- It is now time to deepen your relaxation. Roll your eyes back in your head gently and visualize yourself at the top of a staircase.
- Descent down the stairs slowly, taking one stair at a time. With each stair take a slow, deep breath and let yourself feel even more relaxed than you did on the previous step, drifting deeper and deeper into your relaxing trance state. Start counting from 10 with each step going down until you get to 1 at the bottom of the staircase.
- Once you reach the bottom of the staircase, start implanting the hypnotic suggestions that best suit your desired goal.

Suggestions for weight loss

"I am worthy of having a healthy body and am worthy of being happy with how I look. I lose body fat safely and easily. I program my body and mind to change my body composition now so that I reduce my weight and become leaner each day. My body muscles increase now each day so that I can appear lean and attractive. I am becoming leaner now, my energy is increasing and I feel stronger and more important. I am comfortable and I will now move faster. As my body becomes leaner, I will become healthier. I will feel more confident as I am leaner. I deserve to feel and look good.

"I am a happy, confident person who is happy with my body. I see myself fitting into my smaller size clothes better. My body shape is more pleasing now. My self-esteem is high now. I see myself being active in everything that I do. The fat is still melting off me and I feel lighter.

"I imagine looking at my leaner image in a mirror. My body looks great. I imagine wearing new clothes that I just bought to fit my new body shape. I look good at them. I am so delighted by my body shape. My waist is smaller. I admit I look sexier with my current body composition. All the curves on my body are just in the right place. I look so good. I feel good seeing how lean and beautiful I look. It makes me feel free.

"I feel so in love with myself. I have peace of mind. I don't need food to feel comfortable. I no longer need to isolate myself from other people. I feel protected and secure by myself, and this feeling makes me eat the right foods in the right proportions.

"I will use food to nourish and fuel my body not to reward or entertain myself. Food is like fuel for my body. I will no longer use it to compensate for anything. I will fuel my body with the right food. So I stop myself from eating junk foods that could slow down my body. I will consume nutritious foods.

"Day by day I am losing weight and becoming beautiful and leaner. I feel safe and comfortable with my new appearance. I feel healthy. I feel a sense of freedom as I become healthier and leaner."

(The wake-up)

"I am going to count from 1 to 10. When I reach the number 10, I will be fully awake and alert. I begin. One...awakening from hypnosis. Two...becoming more awake. Three...becoming more conscious. Four...noticing my surroundings. Five...feeling satisfied. Six...feeling safe and comfortable. Seven...feeling more awake and full of health. Eight...looking forward to positive results from this hypnosis session. Nine...feeling wonderful and refreshed. TEN...TEN...TEN...now wide awake and fully alert." (Take a deep breath and then open your eyes. Sit for a moment then stand up slowly)

Script to attract Money

"I have the power and motivation to attract more money. " I now release any limiting beliefs about my ability to make money. I now choose to believe in myself to make more money. I will use this money in a good way. I can have more money and be more generous. I can afford to have the life I want when I have more money.

"I deserve to have anything that I can imagine. I live in a universe that is full of abundance. I allow myself to be a partaker of this abundance. I notice the abundance of wealth and money that is all around me, and I allow myself to flow with that abundance. I accept more money with joy and thanksgiving.

"I am now open to making more money. I see myself holding an immense sum of money. I imagine matching to the ATM to withdraw a vast amount of money. I see myself purchasing a luxurious house and car. I am wise in my decision to make and spend money. I draw the opportunities I need to attract and make more money.

"I can get what I want...yes, I can get what I want. I am smart enough to get anything I want in life. I now foster the thoughts, beliefs, and attitudes necessary to get more money. I now allow creativity and aggressiveness to guide me in generating more money."

(The wake-up)

"I am going to count from 1 to 10. When I reach the number 10, I will be fully awake and alert. I begin. One...starting to awaken from hypnosis. Two...becoming more awake. Three...starting to become more conscious. Four...becoming aware of my surroundings. Five...feeling satisfied. Six...feeling safe and comfortable. Seven...feeling more awake and full of health. Eight...looking forward to positive results from this hypnosis session. Nine...feeling wonderful and refreshed. TEN...TEN...TEN...now wide awake and fully alert." (Take a deep breath and then open your eyes. Sit for a moment then stand up slowly)

Scripts for Happiness

"I deserve to have happiness in all areas of my life. I now feel happy and content. Each day, I am becoming happier and more content. Other people's mistakes are not mine. I choose to be healthy and happy. Life is wonderful in every shape and form. I am now becoming a cheerful person with positive attitudes towards life.

"I will strive to partake of all the goods that come with the world. Every single day, I notice more and more of the good things in my life. The things that make me smile; the things that make me feel good on the inside; things that make me feel proud of myself. And as I notice more of these good things in my life every day, I become happier. As I become happier, it becomes easier for me to see more good things and become happier.

"My spirit is pure and with great joy; it continues to provide me with ultimate happiness. I acknowledge my superpowers and use them to facilitate more happiness. My life is made of joy. I am pure happiness personified."

(The wake-up)

"I am going to count from 1 to 10. When I reach the number 10, I will be fully awake and alert. I begin. One...starting to awaken from hypnosis. Two...becoming more awake. Three...starting to become more conscious. Four...becoming aware of my surroundings. Five...feeling satisfied. Six...feeling safe and comfortable. Seven...feeling more awake and full of health. Eight...looking forward to positive results from this hypnosis session. Nine...feeling wonderful and refreshed. TEN...TEN...TEN...now wide awake and fully alert." (Take a deep breath and then open your eyes. Sit for a moment then stand up slowly)

Script to attract love and relationships

"I deserve love, companionship, compassion, and empathy. The universe loves me and I can find love from the people in it. I can attract ideal people in my love. I release any limiting beliefs and past experiences that prevent me from getting into relationships. I decide now to let go of my feelings of irritation about love and relationships. I am no longer a prisoner of my past.

"I approach relationships with confidence and courage; not seeking what I can get from them, but what I can give to them. There is too much love in my relationship and this brings great joy in my life. I am happy to be in this relationship. I am loved by everyone around me and I continue to love them back in equal measure. I keep nurturing good relationships with the surrounding people. I keep working hard for my relationship. It can work.

"I am in love. I easily attract the right people into my life. I attract positive-minded people and repel those with negative minds. I love the people I attract. I walk a path of light and love. I want to be happy in my relationships. I acknowledge and love the people around me as they love me too."

(The wake-up)

"I am going to count from 1 to 10. When I reach the number 10, I will be fully awake and alert. I begin. One...starting to awaken from hypnosis. Two...becoming more awake. Three...starting to become more conscious. Four...becoming aware of my surroundings. Five...feeling satisfied. Six...feeling safe and comfortable. Seven...feeling more awake and full of health. Eight...looking forward to positive results from this hypnosis session. Nine...feeling absolutely wonderful and refreshed. TEN...TEN...TEN...now wide awake and fully alert." (Take a deep breath and then open your eyes. Sit for a moment then stand up slowly)

Script for Self-love and Confidence

"I love myself. I am so special and there is nobody else like me. I have self-worth and inner beauty. I like who I am and the person I am becoming. My life is so amazing. I love everything about myself. Every day, I grow and become a better version of myself. I praise myself and others naturally and effortlessly.

"I don't need to change anything about myself in order to be accepted and loved. I have a strong belief in myself. People look up to me in everything; they like my character and admire me. I am so grateful for my unique talents, achievements, and health.

"Every day, I am more and more aware of my innate beauty, creativity, and abundance. I am empowered to get the things that I seek. I can assert myself and stand up for myself and others as well. I naturally feel good about myself. Each day, I tap into my greatest potential. Love flows from within me. I love myself for what I am and all that I have accomplished. I believe in myself, my dreams, and my abilities. I am so grateful for everything I have achieved and for what I am yet to do."

(The wake-up)

"I am going to count from 1 to 10. When I reach the number 10, I will be fully awake and alert. I begin. One...starting to awaken from hypnosis. Two...becoming more awake. Three...starting to become more conscious. Four...becoming aware of my surroundings. Five...feeling satisfied. Six...feeling safe and comfortable. Seven...feeling more awake and full of health. Eight...looking forward to positive results from this hypnosis session. Nine...feeling absolutely wonderful and refreshed. TEN...TEN...TEN...now wide awake and fully alert." (Take a deep breath and then open your eyes. Sit for a moment then stand up slowly)

Script for Success

"I want to succeed with all my goals. Success is my portion. I have the determination of a bull and I am wise like an angel. I can succeed in whatever I put my mind to. Nothing can stop me from succeeding, no matter what comes my way. I am motivated to succeed. I know that success is achievable, and I am designed for it. I take action to open doors in my life.

"I know what I want in life, and I will go for it; I dare to put my mind and body to work for it. I now call upon allied forces to aid me in my quest. The universe is already on my side. I have support from all sides: above and below, left and right, in front and behind me.

"I remain silent about my goals. I will only share with those ready to assist me in achieving them directly. I know what I want, I don't need everyone's suggestions and comments. I believe I can have and achieve what I want. I remain silent about my goals until I achieve them.

"Nothing happens unless I make it happen. I will go towards success as it comes towards me. I take my next step towards achieving my ultimate goal. I see myself taking the next step."

(The wake-up)

"I am going to count from 1 to 10. When I reach the number 10, I will be fully awake and alert. I begin. One...starting to awaken from hypnosis. Two...becoming more awake. Three...starting to become more conscious. Four...becoming aware of my surroundings. Five...feeling satisfied. Six...feeling safe and comfortable. Seven...feeling more awake and full of health. Eight...looking forward to positive results from this hypnosis session. Nine...feeling absolutely wonderful and refreshed. TEN...TEN...TEN...now wide awake and fully alert." (Take a deep breath and then open your eyes. Sit for a moment then stand up slowly)

Chapter Five: Powerful Affirmations for Self-Improvement

Repeat the following affirmations three times every day for twenty-one days and see the change that comes your way.

Affirmations for Happiness

I deserve to be happy, and therefore I choose happiness

Today, I create peace, harmony, and joy in my heart

All my previous negative thoughts and self-images have disappeared

Other people's mistakes are not mine

I deserve to have happiness in all areas of my life

I am happy and calm right at this moment

I choose to be happy, feel happy, and have happy thoughts

I give up all negative thoughts and feelings about me

I have everything that I need to be happy about right now

From now henceforth, happiness is my constant state of mind

I am proud of what I have become

I choose to surround myself with happy people

I welcome all the good things the universe offers me

I am so grateful to the universe for all the blessings and good things in my life

From now on, everything is well, and my dreams are coming true every day

Living fully and freely is my birthright

Happiness is a choice, so I choose it

Being happy is becoming my habit day by day

Every time I breathe, I inhale the energy of happiness

My spirit is of great joy, and it continues to provide me with ultimate happiness.

Affirmations for Manifesting Money

Money is a tool that can fully change my life for better

I am worthy of financial security and all that this brings to me

I am magnetizing money and wealth to me in all forms and from all possible sources

Money flows to me effortlessly in various ways

Money is flowing into my life in large quantities from multiple sources NOW

I graciously accept the money that is flowing to me NOW

I expect more money to flow into my life in unexpected ways NOW

I am open and ready to receive more money from all sources NOW

I welcome large sums of money into my life regularly

The negative emotions about money do not serve my financial goals

I set my financial goals because I know I can achieve them

I am on the path to a wealthy life, poverty is not my portion

I have all it takes to be a financially successful person

I do not have any financial worries

Money is flowing to me like a river

I see my bank account figures increasing every single day

Every day I wake up, I get richer and richer

I am thankful for all the money that is present in my life now

Affirmations for Love

I am worthy of love and respect

I trust the universe, and I allow it to help me find genuine love

I give love and it is returned to me multiplied many times

My heart is always open to love

Everywhere I go, I naturally find love

I am surrounded by love; it is all around me

My thoughts are always loving, and my heart is full of love

Today I bless my being with infinite love

Every day my love grows stronger

My belief in love opens my heart to receiving it

All the love I need is within me

Today I choose to be loved and happy

I attract love easily and effortlessly

I deserve to be loved, and I allow myself to be loved

I am a magnet to love,

The more love I give, the more love I receive

Everything I do is in the vibration of love

I give unconditional love to everyone

My heart is filled with love

I deserve love, and I get it in abundance

As I share love with others, the universe gives back love to me

Today I free myself from fear of love, and I open my heart to welcome love

Positive Affirmations for Self-love

I love myself unconditionally

I choose myself today and forever

I respect and love myself for who I am

I embrace self-love as it flows through me

I deserve love; I know that self-love allows others to love me.

I am so proud of myself and my personal journey

I am beautiful in and out

I will stop apologizing for being myself

I am successful and I appreciate what I have in life right now

I am grateful for all my achievements and the gifts in my life

I am stronger because of my struggles

I have an open and loving heart

I am superior to negative thoughts and low actions

Many people look up to me and recognize my worth; I am admired.

I am enthusiastic, energetic and strong

I have the power to create the change I want in my life

I have a beautiful and healthy body, a brilliant mind, and tranquil soul

I have endless and unique talents that I begin to utilize from today

I have all the qualities needed in order to be extremely successful

I completely accept what I cannot change

I am so creative, talented, and original

Powerful Affirmations for Relationships

I attract lasting and happy relationships into my life

I naturally attract perfect relationships into my life

I only attract healthy relationships

My relationships are created in infinite love

I am now ready to accept a happy and lasting relationship

I appreciate every person I meet as worthy as my lover

I am attracting the right person for me

I deserve to be happy in my relationship

I trust the universe that it knows what kind of relationship I need in my life

I am in a wonderful relationship with people who treat me right

I deserve good people around me

All my connections are my significant and they fill me up

I practice and show kindness to everyone around me

My relationships are always fulfilling

I am grateful for the people I have in my life right now

I choose to surround myself only with people who are positive and who lift my energy

I am worth of the real relationship filled with love and respect

I deserve mind-blowing passion in my relationships

I am worth of a healthy, loving relationship

I am grateful for all the love and wonderful relationships in my life

Affirmations for Weight Loss

I deserve to be in perfect body shape

I deserve to have a slim, healthy and attractive body

I am clear about my fitness goals

I choose to embrace thoughts of confidence in my ability to for positive changes in my life

My body has an ideal weight and I have the perfect body shape

I am happy with every part I do in my significant efforts to lose weight

I am committed to my weight loss goal by changing my diet and eating habits from unhealthy to healthy.

I eat the right food for my body and I enjoy healthy food

It is exciting to discover my unique food for weight loss

My metabolism is running optimally, helping me achieve the body weight I desire

Every day I am getting slimmer, leaner and healthier

I exercise every day to enjoy a strong, toned body. I love the feeling exercise gives me

I am getting fitter, tonner and stronger everyday through exercise

I choose to exercise more and more

I am patient with creating my desired body shape and size

I look forward to achieving my ideal weight

I now clearly see myself at my ideal weight and body shape

Positive Affirmations for Success

I deserve to be successful

I am a strong person who attracts success

I am a magnet for success

I succeed in everything that I put my mind on

I have a healthy body, a brilliant mind and a tranquil soul

Everything that is happening in my life now is happening for my ultimate good

My potential to succeed is infinite

I am surrounded by supportive people who believe in me and want me to be successful

I have a limitless ability to conquer all the challenges I encounter

I have the potential to achieve great things in my life

I let go of all old, negative thoughts and beliefs that have stood in the way of my success

I choose to have positive thoughts and create wonderful and successful life that I want

The universe is full of abundance, I am prepared to receive success in abundance

I am passionate about constantly being better and more successful

I continue to climb higher for there is no limit to what I can achieve

Whatever I want comes to me when I go after it

I am so happy because all of my dreams are coming true

Great things are coming my way

I am successful in all areas of my life

Affirmations work when you continually remind your mind what you want to achieve. We live hectic lives that we even forget what we want in life and when opportunities present themselves, we often miss them because we are too busy to notice. To ensure that your affirmations work:

- State your affirmations in the positive
- Have faith. Convince your mind that you have it already
- Repeat your affirmations daily for at least 21 days or until you achieve your desired goal. People believe that it takes 21 days to develop a habit.
- Say your affirmations one at a time with enthusiasm.

Conclusion

The law of attraction through guided meditation, hypnosis and use of affirmations trains you to release the power that is within you. This technique is as old as humankind, yet a few have availed themselves of its benefits. This book teaches you how to use the law of attraction intelligently so that you, too, can realize your full potential in life and achieve your desired goals.

Self-hypnosis, guided meditation, and the use of positive affirmations can contribute positively to every phase of your life — physically, mentally, and spiritually. Do not make the mistake of our ancestors by underestimating the power of utilizing the law of attraction in these forms.

Using hypnosis and guided meditation to enhance life can be wonderful. Just from a suggestion, the mind can mold and create mental interpretations of sensations in ways that they had not been felt before. You can taste colors, feel textures, feel sounds, smell, and enhance the strength of a sensation far greater than you have before. The time has come for the law of attraction to come out of the closet. In your quest for self-improvement, you must try something different.

Key Takeaways

- Set a regular time every day to play or recite the scripts
- A quiet and peaceful place that is free from noise and distractions is these exercises
- Ensure that you are comfortable. Take a posture that makes you more comfortable.
- Release all the tension from your muscles before you start.
- Make well use of hypnosis induction scripts
- To maximize the effect, always repeat the suggestions frequently

- Have strong faith. Convince your subconscious mind that your goal is already a reality.
- Always use visualizations by mental movies to establish goals and empower yourself
- Ensure that you are filled with enthusiasm before starting any of these sessions
- Sometimes, it is natural for your conscious mind to wander during hypnosis or meditation sessions. Don't be concerned that you are wasting time and start blaming yourself, instead, keep focusing.
- Hypnosis, meditation, or rather the law of attraction, can be induced by anyone. It is not meant for specific persons.
- Never force yourself to enter a meditation or hypnosis session. Allow the willingness to come naturally. Vigorous efforts to enter these sessions prevent a successful response as much as strong resistance.
- Words have power, be careful of every word that comes from your mouth.
- Work on one goal or issue at a time.
- The more determined you are to attain a goal, the greater your chances of success
- To be the best subject to these techniques, you have to be more strong-willed, intelligent, and imaginative.

Most successful, powerful, wealthy, and famous people you hear of have used the law of attraction to be where they are. Motivation, discipline, persistence, and psychic empowerment are the most valuable qualities you can possess. Once this is established, solving problems is easy. Using guided meditation, self-hypnosis, and positive affirmations is the quickest and easiest road to your personal and professional growth. They are proven and natural methods for resolving problems quickly and easily.

You can achieve all your goals, change your life, and custom design your destiny using the simple exercises presented throughout this book. You don't need to rely on drugs and health professionals to treat your issues. Try these simple time-tested techniques to solve your problems.

Master Meditation and The Law of Attraction

Introduction to Meditation, Hypnosis & Affirmation Techniques to Learn the Secret of Attracting Wealth, Health, Love, Success, Positivity and More!

Olivia Clifford

Introduction

"Your calm mind is the ultimate weapon against your challenges" - Bryant McGill (Goodreads, n.d.-a).

There are a few terms that you must define for yourself before beginning your practice.

1. **Happiness**

The Merriam-Webster dictionary defines *happiness* as a state of well-being and contentment and goes further to list synonyms including blessedness, bliss, gladness, joy, and warm fuzzies (Merriam-Webster, n.d.-a)

Although happiness can be defined by the terms mentioned above, it's important to acknowledge the subjectiveness of it all. A lunch outing with your family could bring you an immense feeling of happiness and joy, while someone else might find their family unbearable, and spending time with them might bring that person unhappiness and despair. Many people describe happiness as being satisfied with life or the feeling of positive emotions, but it's also important to acknowledge that you can live a happy life while still experiencing moments of sadness.

You see, happiness and sadness go hand in hand. If you've never experienced sadness, then how would you know when the sadness no longer lingers and when happiness creeps in?

I'm sure you've heard the phrase "happiness comes from within," which ties the feeling of happiness with self-confidence, self-belief, self-esteem, and self-image. In addition, many psychologists suggest that being happy is a choice that you can control with your perception of situations and how you respond in these situations (Ackerman, 2019).

These are some of the aspects that you'll learn to focus on when meditating for a greater sense of happiness, but before you can begin, make sure that you know what happiness means to you or at least have a general idea.

When defining happiness for yourself, focus on your intention. A positive intention has been shown to bring more happiness than simply wanting more. Let's break this down a little. If you've decided that buying that multimillion-dollar house will bring you happiness and you want to meditate on this idea, ask yourself why you think this will bring you happiness before beginning your meditation. What is your intention behind buying this house? Do you want the house because you feel like your family deserves it after standing by you through thick and thin? Do you feel like they will have a better quality of life in this setting or do you want the house to drop it in conversation and flaunt the fact that you can afford it? The intention behind your actions, aspirations, and goals are vital when applying the law of attraction, which is outlined in the first chapter. Having positive and good intentions that will positively impact the lives of others and are known to have more positive outcomes and be more sustainable (Kirk, 2019).

While talking about intention, let's quickly cover the topic of money.

The guided meditation and affirmations in this book are based on the law of attraction. Once again, your intention behind meditating to improve your financial success should be defined before your practice. The more positive your intentions, the more positive the outcome of your practice. Now, it's important to realize that meditating to increase financial success won't make you a billionaire overnight. Neither will meditating for love bring you a lover, nor meditating for weight loss make you thinner in a week. Meditation and hypnosis work on one's self to increase personal development and growth so that your goals and aspirations become more attainable as time goes by.

2. **Wealth**

The Merriam-Webster dictionary defines wealth as an abundance of valuable material possessions or resources (Merriam-Webster, n.d.-c).

Once again, the subjectiveness of wealth is important. A man living in a two-bedroom house with his wife and two daughters can have all the wealth that he desires while a man living in a mansion with his wife and son can be constantly searching for more. When using the law of attraction and meditation for wealth, it is important, once again, to define your intention behind your desire.

3. **Well-Being**

According to the Merriam-Webster dictionary, well-being refers to a state of being happy, healthy, or prosperous. (Merriam-Webster, n.d.-d)

When usually thinking of health, the absence of illness comes to mind. Someone who is physically able, strong, and well-looking is said to be in good health, but this is a common misconception.

You see, the World Health Organization (WHO) defined health as "a state of complete physical, mental and social well-being and not merely the absence of disease or infirmity" (WHO, 2019).

This definition was adopted in 1948 and has not been amended since, although there has been talk of the addition of economic or financial well-being to the definition. So, from this definition, it is possible to conclude that mental and social well-being play just as big a role in health as the physical aspect.

With this in mind, a physically disabled man with an amputated leg, unable to move without the aid of his wheelchair, could have a great level of mental and social health and still live a happy and healthy life. This man could be said to be healthier than the old lady a couple of doors away who looks physically fit but lacks the coping mechanisms to deal with her rude daughter-in-law and has recently shied away from social interaction with her friends for the same reason.

4. Love

The Merriam-Webster dictionary defines love as a strong affection for another arising out of kinship or personal ties, affection based on admiration, common interests, or attraction based on sexual desires (Merriam-Webster, n.d.-b)

When it comes to any relationship, be it romantic, family, or friends, it's usually easier to find fault in the other person when something goes wrong. The meditation techniques using the law of affirmation that are outlined in this book describes the importance of self-reflecting and being true to yourself when interacting with others. It's important to ensure that you're ready for a relationship before diving into one headfirst, whether it's a new friendship or more romantic. Family relationships are usually much more difficult to deal with while it's easy to simply run away from people you don't have blood ties with. That's where meditation and the power of calming your mind comes in!

Now that you've got a general understanding of the definitions above, let's get into it!

Chapter 1: The Law of Attraction

"Once you make a decision, the universe conspires to make it happen" - Ralph Waldo Emerson (Ralph Waldo Emerson Quotes, n.d.-a).

Basically, the law of attraction states that you'll attract into your life what you focus on. Whatever you put your energy into will manifest and come back to you in a positive way.

The widely accepted dogma in the law of attraction is that "like attracts like." Let me break it down for you.

The law of attraction is based on energy, focus, and intention. Positive energy is associated with feelings, thoughts, and actions that are positive. This may include feelings of happiness, joy, compassion, and gratitude. Thoughts that bring about these feelings as well as those that draw your focus to your goals and the things that are important to you are also positive. Lastly, your actions that are in keeping with your positive thoughts and feelings are naturally positive. Generally, positivity is associated with good.

Any of your thoughts, actions, and feelings that give you a sense of happiness and positivity, usually work *for* you in building your life and give you a positive sense of well-being. Thoughts, actions, and feelings that work *against* you in achieving your goals and aspirations are usually classified as "bad" and are associated with negative energy. For example, consistent thoughts of anger, lashing out at the people you love, or even snoozing that alarm clock one too many times every morning could be a few examples. Anger always leaves you feeling worse than you started, and lashing out at the ones you love makes everyone unhappy. These things work *against* you in building a happy life of positive well-being. Snoozing that alarm clock one too many times, although a meager action compared to the anger, also works *against* you in building your life because it allows you to slip into the bad habit of waking up late which will then impact your punctuality, leading to a bad professional reputation and maybe eventually make you unemployable. I know this seems a little extreme, but that's what happens when you let negative energy and bad habits grow out of control like that.

The energy that you give out is the energy that you'll receive. Now, this book is written in the context of living a happier and healthier life and using the law of attraction to help you reach your aspirations and build a life of happiness and positive well-being. Of course, there is no light without the dark, so there is no positivity without negativity, and each has its part to play. Negative feelings and thoughts can't be banished, never to be seen or heard of again, but the way you react to these feelings and thoughts can be positive and is very much in your control.

Positive energy attracts positive energy; negative energy attracts negative energy. Have you ever noticed how one success usually spearheads a whole series of successes and victories? That, my friend, is the law of attraction. The initial success left you feeling so positive and inspired that you began emitting a sense of positivity that the universe responded to, sending more positivity your way! What about the way anger or fear seems to compound in certain situations? Again, you begin emitting a negative energy that attracts more negativity toward yourself.

This means that you can manifest certain aspirations or outcomes by having positive intentions and practicing techniques that allow you to experience and emit more positivity. Whatever energy you're creating will determine how the universe responds to you and the opportunities that will present themselves to you.

Whatever you're thinking, feeling, and doing at any given time creates vibrations in the form of energy that will attract the energy of the same frequency i.e., positive or negative (Canfield, 2019).

Knowing that you're mostly in control of the energy you emit is not enough to use the power of the law of attraction to your advantage. In addition to your energy frequencies and intentions being in tune with your system of values and beliefs, you need to also consciously create a better life for yourself in the process. You can do this by:

- Choosing how to react in certain situations
- Choosing to challenge your thoughts that bring about negative emotions and feelings
- Choosing to spend your time doing things that make you happy and feel positive
- Choosing to adjust your lifestyle and habits so that they are in keeping with your intentions, values, and beliefs
- Choosing to be open-minded and objective when the situation calls for it
- Choosing to practice gratitude and focusing on all that you have instead of all that you don't have

The process of consciously creating a better life for yourself requires a well-known practice called mindfulness which goes hand-in-hand with meditation and positive living.

Mindfulness

"The present moment is the only time over which we have dominion. Live the actual moment. Only this actual moment is life" - Thich Nhat Hanh (Goodreads, n.d.-b).

Mindfulness is the ability to be fully present and aware of your internal and external environments. Your internal environment includes your thoughts, feelings, and emotions, all of which you have a certain degree of control over. This environment also includes your perceptions and perspectives, your opinions, and the choices you make before you carry out your actions. Your external environment refers to the things around you that you have no control over. These include other people's opinions, the weather, the traffic, the stock markets, and the like. You do, however, have control of how to respond to situations in your external environment, and this makes all the difference.

Practicing mindfulness will allow you to identify experiences that leave with negative feelings and thus attracting more negativity. This way, you can modify these experiences to make them more positive or even avoid these experiences altogether. Let's look at a simple example. Your wife insists that you go out with all of her friends' husbands for a guy's night once a month. The day arrives, and there are four of you in total. You have nothing in common with the other husbands, and although you try to involve yourself in the conversation, it feels forced and inorganic. You feel a sense of pressure and anxiety when interacting with them, and you can tell that they feel it, too. Being mindful of your thoughts, feelings, and body language in this situation will tell you that the energy you're emitting is not exactly positive. You're anxious, a little on edge, annoyed that you're unable to hold a decent conversation, and a little stressed because you really want to make this work to make your wife happy. At the end of the experience, you head home and assess the night. The truth is, you had a terrible time, and you would have been much happier just staying home and spending time with your wife. That would have improved your mood and conversation and you would have felt more comfortable, resulting in an overall positive experience. Now you have to decide whether it's in the best interest of you and your wife if you continue to go out with the guys once a month.

Worst-case scenario is that you'll keep going out with them, and slowly but surely you would begin to resent your wife for forcing you to do it in the first place. Best case-scenario is that you sit down and have a conversation with your wife about the fact that you tried but you just don't feel comfortable going out with those guys every month. It isn't anything they did or said, they just aren't your type of people, and that's okay. Then, you might end up using that time to attend a monthly cooking class with your wife which will leave you feeling happy and fulfilled, and it will positively influence your sense of well-being.

When aiming to live a more positive life, it's important to still remember that negative experiences have their place, and sometimes discomfort is required for growth. Being mindful should also come with complete honesty with yourself about your experiences. Let's take learning how to swim, for example. You may feel like you're drowning sometimes and a sense of complete discomfort in the icy water, but keeping in mind the intention behind the experience can help you maintain a positive mindset that will counteract these experiences. For example, you may say to yourself, "It might feel like I'm drowning sometimes, but not for much longer. Soon I'll be able to swim!" or even "The water may be icy, but these few moments of discomfort are worth me learning how to swim!"

Using the Law of Attraction

The energy that you emit comes from your thoughts, feelings, and actions, so every moment of every day there are vibrations that are being sent out from your being. To control your mind every second of every day would be an extremely taxing process, and the focus required will prevent you from living life to the fullest. It is important not to become obsessive about your thoughts and feelings. You'll find that small everyday changes, like those described in a later chapter, can positively impact the way you experience life and when regularly practiced can become somewhat of a habit.

First things first, when using the law of attraction to reach your goals and aspirations, it's important to be intentional about them. Clearly define your goal and the reason you want to achieve it. Then ask yourself the following questions:

1. Why do I want to achieve my goal?
2. What are the steps I need to take to get closer to this goal?
3. How long do I think it will take me to achieve this goal?
4. Once I achieve this goal, how do I intend to sustain it?

Be completely honest with yourself when asking these questions. Once you have defined your goal and the intention behind it, you may start your visualization process.

Visualization

"Visualization is daydreaming with a purpose" - Bo Bennett (Bo Bennett Quotes, n.d.).

Visualization techniques are essential in using the law of attraction to achieve your goals. Being able to see or imagine your aspirations within reach will keep you inspired and motivated as well as allow you to emit positive energy.

You may visualize yourself achieving your goal and imagine the feelings and emotions that will come with the achievement. Imagine the exact scene from the clothes that you're wearing to the people you want to share the moment with.

Creating a vision board that you can display in a visible area will also remind you of your goals and the positive feelings that it brings. However, visualizing the end goal is just as important as visualizing how to get there.

Focus on and talk about or journal what you want to manifest your goals. Don't focus on what you don't want! Maintain a sense of positivity and inspiration by remembering your intention behind the goal.

After you have an idea about how to go about achieving your goal and you've been focusing on what you want to achieve in a positive light, take action to bring you closer to your aspiration. Remember, the law of attraction doesn't work if you don't! Believe that you're going to achieve your goals and understand that if you don't, it means that there was something better meant for you.

Attach positive emotions and feelings to your goals and aspirations and set yourself daily reminders to journal or even just think about what you wish to achieve. Speak these thoughts into the universe to manifest your goals while taking action to achieve them.

As Ralph Waldo Emerson said, "A man is what he thinks about all day long." (Ralph Waldo Emerson Quotes, n.d.-b).

Chapter 2: Meditation and Hypnosis

Meditation

"Learn to be calm and you will always be happy" – Paramahansa Yogananda ("Learn to be calm and you will always be happy," n.d.).

Meditation is a daily practice that allows you to sit quietly and still your mind so that you may experience a sense of calm and relaxation. There are various techniques and ways in which you can meditate, but ultimately, the goal of meditation is to nourish the mind like we nourish the body: daily.

Throughout our lives, we are constantly moving, both body and mind, and focusing on getting from one place to the next. Be it getting from home to work or maybe getting from working as an assistant to working as a manager, the point is, we are constantly looking to where we can go next. Meditation is a practice that allows you to be still and, at the moment, as you slow down a little and be mindful of all that you have, while still giving some attention to what you wish to accomplish.

Mindfulness meditation, originating from Buddhist teachings, is the most commonly practiced form of meditation in the Western world and incorporates being completely aware of your body, mind, and external environment as you repeat a mantra, allowing your mind to settle and be completely present in the moment.

Meditative practices have been shown to improve daily focus, reduce anxiety, increase creativity, improve memory and cognitive functioning, as well as increase compassion and feelings of positivity among individuals (Cooper, 2013).

The use of meditation in the achievement of goals and aspirations has been practiced for centuries. Being mindful of your intentions and aspirations during the meditative process has been associated with feelings of positivity and calm that contribute to the positive energy that is emitted from an individual.

Hypnosis

"The easier you can make it inside your head, the easier it will make things outside your head" - Richard Bandler (n.d.).

More commonly, "hypnosis is a state of extreme self-focus and attention in which minimal attention is given" to the external environment, unlike in meditation where the external environment is observed as well (Lumen, n.d.). This trance-like state showcases heightened focus and concentration and leaves the individual in a suggestible mood. Being open to suggestions can help you gain control of undesirable behaviors as well as allow you to consider changes in your lifestyle that may benefit you positively (Mayo Clinic, 2018).

Myths About Hypnosis

There are a few myths and misunderstandings associated with hypnosis and hypnotherapy that are important to iron out before going any further (HMI College of Hypnotherapy, 2004):

1. Hypnosis involves mind control.

This is absolutely incorrect! No one can control your mind unless you let them. Hypnosis simply induces a suggestible state that will allow your mind to be more open to changes that will positively influence your well-being. Your subconscious mind will reject all suggestions that you don't agree with or don't understand. You can specify exactly what suggestions you want your hypnotherapist to feed your superconscious mind while being hypnotized.

2. Hypnosis will allow someone else to control my body.

Once again, not true! This assumption is based on Hollywood fiction, mostly. Although your mind is in a suggestible state, allowing yourself to partake in serious suggestions about your self-improvement will not leave you barking like a dog or walking like a duck.

3. If I can be hypnotized, it means that my mind is weak.

This belief, although common throughout most of history, has actually been scientifically proven as untrue. The most important aspect of hypnotism is the willingness to be induced into a suggestible state of mind. Going into a hypnotherapist's room with a closed mind is not going to give you the results you desire. Even war veterans, who have been trained in the psychology of killing and have the mental strength exceed that of an average civilian, have been hypnotized in the treatment of post-traumatic stress disorder (PTSD).

4. If I'm hypnotized, I will have no memory of it.

Hypnosis is not an unconscious state of sleep; it's actually associated with hyperawareness, heightened concentration and focus, and increased sensitivity of the senses.

5. I might not be able to snap out of it if I'm hypnotized.

Coming out of hypnosis is similar to coming out of meditation, to be quite honest. Simply stretching or gently opening your eyes can naturally allow you to transcend out of the hypnotic state.

6. Hypnosis will cause amnesia.

Only a very small percentage of people who undergo hypnosis go into a deep enough level or state that may cause spontaneous amnesia. The vast majority of individuals remember everything from their hypnotic experiences and may even experience enhancements in memory.

Self-Hypnosis

Self-hypnosis, involving no external party, like the guide provided in this book, is significantly more affordable than a weekly hypnotherapist appointment and can provide very similar results. In addition, you have access to the guide whenever you need it and can practice as often as you like in the comfort and privacy of your own home.

Although the self-hypnosis guide in this book is a general guide that can be modified as specified, it is also possible for you to adopt the guide to other specific issues that you may require help with. There is an additional guideline on how to adapt the guide to other specific issues included at the end of the guided hypnosis chapter.

Since with self-hypnosis, there is no second party involved, it is important to journal the thoughts and emotions that may arise during your hyperaware state and analyze these thoughts and emotions at a later stage. These analyses may bring to light other issues that may need some attention (St John, 2018).

The more you practice the technique of self-hypnosis, the easier it will become to reach the hypnotic state.

Chapter 3: Affirmations

Affirmations are positive phrases or words that can help you overcome natural negativity and negative thoughts. In addition, these statements can keep you motivated, inspired, and promote an overall feeling of positivity (Mind Tools, 2019).

According to a study done on positive thinking, spending just a few minutes thinking about your positive characteristics and reminding yourself how capable you are and can significantly improve your performance and problem-solving abilities (Kang et al., 2015).

Affirmations and positive self-talk have also recently been used to successfully treat people with low self-esteem and depression, resulting in positive therapeutic outcomes and overall improved quality of life (Peden et al., 2001).

Words have immense power, and affirmations and positive self-talk can positively affect your life by:

- Motivating and inspiring you to put your plans into action
- Helping you remain focused on your goals
- Boosting your self-confidence and self-belief
- Helping improve and maintain relationships
- Improving health and well-being

All of these positive effects essentially improve your energy frequency which results in the emission of positive energy. This in turn, by the law of attraction, results in an increased chance of success and achievement.

The Importance of Touch

Scientific research undertaken on the importance of touch and the effect it has on the human body has shown that touch expresses warmth, trust, and mostly positive emotions (Schwartz, 2016).

The research has shown that basic warm touch calms cardiovascular stress, even when one uses their own palms to warm their own shoulders. When stressed or sad, you might find yourself curling up into the fetal position on your bed, rocking your body back and forth. Researchers suggest that this position is ideal for stress management, as it allows most of your body to be in contact with another part, spreading the warmth and the feeling of safety.

In the same way, while practicing aspirations, patting your chest or touching your forehead can increase the positive experience of this practice. For example, sit comfortably and gently close your eyes. Once your eyes are closed, breathe in and out, simply calming your mind. Then start to say your affirmation out loud. While you say your affirmation, bring one of your palms to your chest and gently pat your chest. Pat your chest as you repeat, "I love myself because I am me".

Designing Affirmations

Now that you have an understanding of what affirmations are, let's have a look at how to design your own affirmations that are specific to you.

A couple of tips when designing affirmations are as follows:

1. Always create the affirmation in the present tense. Starting with the words, "I am" is usually a good way to go.
2. Always state the affirmation in a positive way. For example, instead of, "I am not weak and scared," rather say, "I am strong and courageous."
3. Make your affirmations specific to your goals. For example, if your goal is to be a world-class swimmer you might say, "I will swim 50 meters in under 25 seconds."
4. If you find yourself stuck at a negative thought, use the word "but" to change the narrative. For example, "I am overweight

and struggling with my exercise routine, but I am still here, and I am still trying."

Remember, using the law of attraction and positivity will not have you achieving your goals overnight. You still need to work for what you want to achieve!

Examples of Affirmations

Although this book contains guided meditations and hypnosis for love, money, weight loss, relationships, and happiness, there are many other aspects of your life that you can assess and address with meditation and hypnosis to ultimately experience positive outcomes.

Affirmations come into play during the meditation or hypnosis where you may want to repeat them as mantras or even just as daily reminders or inspiration.

Now, as mentioned earlier in this book, self-development and self-awareness are both a large part of living happy and healthy. Looking to develop one's self instead of looking externally to blame others for negative experiences is a large part of the growth process and can positively impact your well-being and quality of life. As a result, each of the following sections will also contain affirmations aimed at you, the individual, and your self-development.

Powerful Affirmations for Love

1. I deserve to find love.
2. My heart is open for love.
3. I have more love to give than I ever thought possible.
4. I am surrounded by love.

5. I love my spouse.
6. I deserve to be loved the way my spouse loves me.
7. My love is unconditional.
8. I love without restraint.
9. Someone out there deserves my love.
10. I will find the one who deserves my love.
11. I am attracting love.
12. I have love within me.
13. I am grateful for the love that I have.
14. The more I love myself, the more I love my partner.
15. I deserve happiness.
16. I am open to love.
17. I give and receive love.
18. I believe in my ability to love.
19. When I am ready for love, love will find me.
20. I am thankful that the universe will help me find love.
21. I will allow love to find me easily.
22. I am ready for love to find me.
23. I can love, so I can be loved.
24. I trust my partner completely.
25. I let love flow into my life.
26. I am building my life with love.
27. I share my life with my love.
28. Life is full of love.
29. I will be my true love's love.
30. I will attract my best friend in a lover.

Powerful Affirmations for Financial Success

1. Money flows toward me.
2. I am worthy of the money that is coming my way.
3. There is always more than enough money in my life.
4. I deserve to be paid for my skills.
5. I am wealthy in so many ways.
6. I am grateful for the abundance of wealth that I possess.
7. I am worthy of the richness I desire.
8. I am aligned with my purpose.
9. What's meant for me is coming.

10. I am aligned with the energy of abundance.
11. I will boldly conquer my financial goals.
12. I humbly accept and receive the money that is coming toward me.
13. I am growing into someone who is financially successful.
14. I am learning the skills required to make me financially successful.
15. I am in control of my success.
16. I will be successful, maybe not immediately but indefinitely.
17. I am responsible for my financial success.

Powerful Affirmations for Weight Loss

1. I deserve good health.
2. I am going to lose weight and achieve my goals.
3. I am listening to what my body needs from me.
4. I am pushing my body to its limits.
5. I am transforming my lifestyle into something healthier.
6. I am making small and sustainable changes that will benefit me in the long run.
7. I feel happier and healthier.
8. I am active and full of energy.
9. I choose to nourish my body in a healthy way.
10. I am fitter today than I was yesterday.
11. I nourish my body with what I feed it.
12. I think before I eat.
13. I am moving forward each day.
14. I breathe in relaxation and breathe out stress.
15. I am drinking water to regulate my mood and metabolism.
16. I crave mindfulness more than I crave sweet treats.
17. I am on a path of wellness.
18. I love my body.
19. I value self-control and self-mastery.
20. I will control my impulses and cravings.
21. I wake up each day with determination.
22. I strengthen my own self-mastery by resisting temptation.
23. I am strong enough to achieve this goal.
24. I acknowledge that not all thoughts need to be acted on.

25. I challenge my existing beliefs.
26. I make peace with the past.
27. I find new hope in every new day.
28. I am capable of discipline.
29. I am healthy.
30. I can lose weight easily.
31. I am patient with myself and my body.

Powerful Affirmations for Relationships

1. I am surrounded by love and acceptance.
2. I love and accept those around me.
3. I attract good, kind, and loving people into my life.
4. I welcome kindness and love with open arms.
5. I appreciate all the people I have in my life.
6. My partner and I love each other.
7. My partner and I laugh every day.
8. I feel happy in my partner's presence.
9. Our love is stronger than arguments.
10. Love always wins.
11. I go through life with the help of my loved ones.
12. I am ready to accept a happy, fulfilling relationship.
13. I deserve the happiness that my loved ones bring me.
14. I love myself to the fullest.
15. Love is all around me, and I am worthy of it.
16. I am surrounded by love.
17. I attract loving people into my life because I am loving.
18. I appreciate all that I am.
19. I am good enough the way I am.
20. I am still growing and changing as time goes by.
21. I am becoming better for the ones that I love.
22. I am working on being able to communicate more openly.
23. I will be able to communicate more openly.
24. I am nonjudgmental toward others just as I am toward myself.
25. I release all desperation and allow love to find me.

Powerful Affirmations for Happiness

1. I have the power to shape my ideal reality.
2. I create the life I want with my good intentions.
3. When I feel happy, I manifest more reasons to be happy.
4. I am happy right now.
5. I am worthy of feeling happy.
6. My happiness comes from within me.
7. There are so many positives in my life.
8. I am so grateful for the happiness that I have.
9. I experience so much joy in the things that I do.
10. I allow myself to feel happy and good.
11. My choice to be happy keeps me healthy.
12. I am meant to live a happy life.
13. My inner joy overflows into my life and allows me to share this feeling with others.
14. I am grateful to be alive.
15. Happiness is my birthright.
16. Good things are happening within me and around me.
17. I feel deeply fulfilled.

Chapter 4: Breathing

The Process of Breathing

When you breathe in or inhale, the muscle just beneath your ribcage, your diaphragm, contracts and moves downward, allowing your lungs more space to expand. The muscles between your ribs, known as your intercostal muscles, contract and push your ribcage upward and outward. As your lungs expand, air travels down your trachea from your nose and your mouth and eventually reaches your lungs. When the air has reached the little air sacs at the end of its journey into your lungs, oxygen from the air you have breathed passes into the bloodstream. At the same time, carbon dioxide passes from your bloodstream into your lungs and is exhaled and released from the body (Elliot, 2017).

Every process in the body relies on oxygen. Your organs need ample oxygen to function properly, so effective breathing can increase your digestion, improve your body's immunity, improve your cognition and memory, and even help you sleep better (Elliot, 2017).

During meditation and when inducing hypnosis, focusing on your breath is important to help you reach a deeper state of consciousness. Different breathing techniques exist that may be practiced with meditation or in isolation, with different benefits in daily life. A few of the techniques are mentioned in this chapter.

Deep Breathing

In everyday life, the shallow breaths that we take while carrying out everyday tasks allow us to take in enough oxygen to ensure that our body and mind are functional. Even though something is functioning doesn't mean that it is functioning optimally or to the best of its ability. Utilizing certain breathing techniques can improve the functionality of the body and mind. Deep breathing is one of these techniques.

Deep breathing, or diaphragmatic breathing, is a technique that is practiced widely with meditation. It focuses on slowing down your breathing and being mindful of the air as it enters and leaves your body.

The benefits of deep breathing or diaphragmatic breathing have been studied in-depth and include (Jewell, 2018):

- Lowering levels of the stress hormone cortisol in your body, thus increasing relaxation
- Improving core muscle stability and balance
- Improving cognitive function and memory
- Improving immunity against infection
- Increasing and improving digestion
- Stimulating the lymphatic system to remove excess toxins from the body
- Increasing energy
- Reducing blood pressure and heart rate

Before getting into a deep breathing exercise, you must practice this technique on an empty stomach or about an hour after a meal. Eating a large meal before practicing can make you feel uncomfortable.

Let's practice deep breathing!

Sit in a comfortable seated position with your back straight. If you're a beginner and are unable to sit cross-legged for long periods, don't beat yourself up: You'll get there if that's what you want. Rather, sit on a chair with a backrest so that your back remains upright to allow for the expansion of your lungs. Allow your hands to gently fall in your lap and close your eyes.

First, breathe in, completely, sucking in as much air as you can through your nose, to the count of three. As you breathe in, expand your chest by sticking it outward and swell out your tummy, allowing your lungs to inflate completely. Be mindful of the breath as it enters your body. Feel the air enter your nose and flow down into your lungs. Notice the temperature of the air as it enters your body. Hold the breath in your lungs for a moment and then slowly breathe out, through your nose or mouth, whichever is more comfortable, to the count of six. While breathing out, ensure that your back remains straight, and as you push all the air out of your lungs, suck in your tummy, feeling your abdominal muscles working as you do. As soon as all the air has been pushed out of your lungs, take a nice deep breath in again, to the count of three. Remember, focus on the breath, feel it going down into your lungs and swell your tummy out to allow your lungs to expand completely, and then hold the breath for a moment. Then slowly release your breath to the count of six, sucking your tummy in to push all the extra air out. Focus on feeling the breath as it enters and leaves your body.

Breathing out for double the count that you breathe in for is an important aspect of deep breathing. This technique stimulates the branch of the nervous system that controls your rest and digest function and therefore improves digestion while allowing you to feel relaxed and rested.

Alternate Nostril Breathing

This type of breath enters and leaves through the nose only and has also shown to have many benefits, including (Art of Living Faculty, 2020):

- Lowering stress and anxiety
- Improving cardiovascular function
- Improving lung capacity
- Improving cognitive function and memory
- Harmonizes the right and left hemispheres of the brain
- Maintains body temperature

Let's breathe!

Sit in a comfortable seated position, once again your back must be straight to allow for maximum expansion of the lungs. Sitting on a chair with a backrest is ideal for beginners. Allow your nondominant hand to gently rest in your lap. If you're right-handed, your left hand will be resting in your lap; if you're left-handed, your right hand will be resting in your lap. In the guide below, the right hand is taken as dominant.

Now, hold your dominant hand in front of you, palm facing you, and fold your middle and pointer finger inward toward your palm. Now, bring your hand to your face and place your index finger over your left nostril and your thumb over your right. Your fingers should be placed so that it is easy to pinch your nose closed.

Close your right nostril with your thumb, releasing your left nostril by lifting your index finger. Breathe in deeply through your left nostril, feeling the breath as it travels down into your lungs, expanding your tummy as you do. When you have taken in as much air as you can, close the left nostril by pinching your nose closed, and hold the breath for a moment. Then, open the right nostril by releasing the thumb and slowly, in a controlled manner, breath out, pushing all the air out of your lungs and sucking your tummy in as you do. While your right nostril is still open, breathe in deeply and completely, feeling the breath in your body and expanding your tummy as you do. Then pinch your nose, closing both nostrils as you hold your breath for a moment. When you're ready to breathe out, release your left nostril by lifting your index finger, and slowly, in a controlled manner, breathe out completely, sucking your tummy in as you do. Then, breathe in through the left nostril again.

Humming & Bumble Bee Breath

This technique allows for the creation of vibrations while exhaling that have been shown to increase nitric oxide (NO) production in the sinuses of the skull. NO from our nose and sinuses is inhaled with every breath we take and works on the blood vessels in the lungs to cause dilation and enhance the body's ability to take up oxygen as well as remove carbon dioxide (Harrold, 2020).

The humming bee breath is a great practice for relaxation and calming as well. The benefits of this technique include (Harrold, 2020):

- Calming the mind
- Boosting the immune system
- Reducing blood pressure
- Regulating metabolism
- Reducing inflammation
- Improving digestion
- Improving memory and decision-making skills

Let's hum like a bee!

Bring yourself into a comfortable seated position with your back straight so that you can expand your lungs completely. Once again, sitting on a chair with a backrest would be perfect. Gently close your eyes, and place your index fingers on your tragus, the cartilage between your ear and your cheek. You may gently rest your face in the palms of your hand to allow your index fingers to rest on the tragus of each ear.

Take a deep breath in, expanding your tummy as you do, feeling the air enter your body. Now, as you breathe out, make a humming sound from your throat while you gently press the tragus of each ear to close the ear. Feel the vibration in your head and the relaxation that comes with it as you breathe out while humming, and suck your tummy in to push all the air out of your lungs. You may repeat this breath as many times as you'd like.

If you're unable to close your ear with your tragus, gently plugging your ear with your index finger works just as well.

Now that we've learned a few breathing techniques, let's meditate!

Chapter 5: Guided Meditation for the Law of Attraction

A Beginner's Guide to Meditation

To start, practice meditating for about 10 minutes a day, then slowly increase the time as you feel comfortable to 10 minutes twice a day. Eventually, you'll find yourself looking forward to your meditation time and may even want to increase it to 20 minutes twice a day.

Sit in a quiet and comfortable space with your back upright and your body relaxed. It's important to be honest with yourself about where you currently are in your journey. You might not be able to sit cross-legged on the floor for long periods, and that's absolutely okay. In order to experience the full benefits of meditation, it's important to be comfortable. Sitting on a chair with a backrest is a great place to start, and as you become more comfortable sitting cross-legged, you may transition into this position as time goes on. Remember, be honest with yourself about your capabilities and your limits. If you find yourself slouching or unable to maintain an upright posture while sitting without a backrest, rather choose to sit on a chair as sitting upright is vital for your lungs to expand to their full capacity. In addition, muscle spasms and cramps can sometimes make it difficult and uncomfortable to meditate if you're unused to sitting in the cross-legged posture for long periods. For this guide, we'll use a chair, but you may feel free to sit in whichever posture you're comfortable in, making sure that your back is straight and upright.

Sit on a chair with your back upright and against the backrest. Place your feet flat on the floor, being mindful not to cross your legs at your ankles or over your knees. Place your hands on your lap with your palms facing up toward the sky. Ensure that your posture is upright and that your chest is open with your eyes looking forward. Your entire body should be relaxed in this posture; there should be no tension in your body. If you're feeling tension in any area, gently stretch that area before meditating to relieve the tension.

Once you're comfortable in your seated position, gently close your eyes and focus on your breath. Breathe in through your nose to the count of three, pushing out your tummy as you inhale, allowing your lungs to expand to full capacity. Feel the air enter your body through your nose, pass through your throat, and down your chest into your lungs. Feel the temperature of the air and the way it cools your nose as it enters your body. Imagine the air as a breath of positivity that you're breathing in to nourish your body. Once your lungs are filled with air, hold the breath for a moment and then gently release the breath through your nose, slowly and in a controlled manner, to the count of six. Push all the air out of your lungs as you suck your tummy in, feeling your abdominal muscles working. As you breathe out, feel the warmth that it brings as you exhale. Feel the air moving as it travels from your lungs up through your chest and throat and through your nose. Imagine that this warm air is like the dark smoke that comes out of a volcano and that you're breathing out all the negativity that has been holding your back. As you sit and focus on your breath, thoughts will come and go. Allow these thoughts to flow by like a river, and simply observe them as they move along. Don't attach a feeling to these thoughts or fixate on any one of them. Simply let them flow.

While sitting in this meditative state and focusing on your breath, you might want to begin thinking of a mantra. Your mantra doesn't have to be religious or spiritual. It can be an affirmation that you want to recite or even words that will improve your mood and sense of well-being like "gratitude" or "happiness." Remember to hold your mantra in your thoughts and not mouth the words physically. Keep your body still and relaxed and focus on your breath.

Your mantra and intentions during your meditation are very important, as these are the things that determine the frequency of energy that you'll emit. In order to emit positive energy so that you may attract the same, your mantra and intentions must in turn be positive. Using meditation and the law of attraction to achieve your goals and aspirations usually has positive outcomes if practiced with the right energy and intention.

When you're ready to end your meditation, let your mantra go, and bring back your focus only to your breath. Sit there for one or two moments and begin to consciously think words of gratitude. You may want to think of phrases such as, "I am grateful for my being" or "I am thankful for all that I am." Then, gently tilt your head downward, bringing your chin to your chest and stretching the back of your neck, as if to bow to the universe. Slowly become aware of your surroundings by wiggling your toes and your fingers. When you're ready, slowly and gently open your eyes and stretch your arms over your head to bring full awareness back to your body.

Meditation for Love

Begin your meditation as laid out in the guide above. Focus on your breath as you sit comfortably; keep your back straight and your eyes gently closed. Breathe in to three counts, feeling the air as it enters your body through your nose and flows into your lungs. Hold the breath for a moment and then slowly exhale, through your nose, in a controlled manner, to the count of six.

As you breathe in, imagine that the air you're breathing is a pink fog that smells like candy floss and rose petals. Feel the air of love enter your body as you inhale. You're attracting love with your intentions and positive energy. Now, as you breathe out, imagine your breath like the smoke of a volcano, breathing out all the negativity that has prevented you from experiencing love in the past. Don't attach emotions to any thoughts that may flow through your mind. Simply focus on your breath and your intention. The universe will bring love to you because of your positive intentions and energy.

As you breathe and focus on your breath, start thinking of an affirmation for love to remind yourself that the law of attraction will bring love to you if you continue with your positive intentions and energy. The affirmation you may want to hold in your mind may be "I am worthy of love" or "I am ready for love." You may want to refer back to the chapter on affirmations and choose one best suited for how you're feeling on this specific day, or you can create your own affirmations or mantras. For example, you might hold the phrase, "Love will come when the time is right" in your mind, and this might become your mantra. Remember, you may change your mantra each time you meditate.

When you're ready to end your meditation, let your mantra flow away and imagine that it is flowing toward the universe so that the universe may understand your intentions. Think thoughts of gratitude such as, "I am grateful that the universe is on my side." Slowly bring your focus back to only your breath. Slowly become aware of your surroundings as you drop your head forward to stretch the back of your neck, bow to the universe, and start to wiggle your toes and fingers. Then when you're ready, gently open your eyes and stretch your arms over your head.

Meditation for Money

Begin your meditation as laid out in the guide above and focus on your breath. As you breathe in, imagine that the air you're breathing is golden and beautiful. Feel the air as it enters your body through your nose and travels to your lungs. Imagine that you're breathing in the wealth that you deserve. As you breathe out, imagine that the air you're exhaling is like the dark ash from a volcano as you breathe out all the negativity within yourself that has held you back from achieving your aspirations. As you sit and breathe, let the thoughts that come to mind flow past like the water in a river. Now begin to think of a mantra or affirmation in your mind. You may want to hold the thought, "All the money that I deserve is on its way to me" or "I am worthy of the wealth that is coming to me." As you repeat this thought in your mind, continue to focus on your breath and your positive intentions behind your aspiration. You're attracting money with your intentions and positive energy.

When you're ready to end your meditation, let your mantra flow away and imagine that it is flowing toward the universe so that the universe may understand your intentions. Think thoughts of gratitude such as, "I am grateful for all that the universe has given me." Slowly bring your focus back to only your breath. Now, become aware of your surroundings as you drop your head forward to stretch the back of your neck, bow to the universe, and start to wiggle your toes and fingers. Then when you're ready, gently open your eyes and stretch your arms over your head.

Meditation for Happiness

Begin your meditation as laid out in the guide above and focus on your breath. As you breathe in, imagine that the air you're breathing is beautifully colored like a rainbow and smells like flowers, freshly baked cookies, and other little things that may make you happy, like your partner's cologne or the smell of your daughter's baby shampoo. Feel the air as it enters your body through your nose and flows into your lungs and imagine the colors from the air radiating from your lungs throughout your body, spreading happiness throughout your being. As you breathe out, imagine that the air you're exhaling is dark ash of all the negativity within you that you're expelling from your being so that what remains is positivity and light. As you sit and focus on your breath, let the thoughts that come flow away, never fixating or attaching emotion to them. Then, as you become comfortable in your breathing, begin to think of a mantra or affirmation with positive energy and the best of intentions. You may want to hold the thought, "I deserve all the happiness that I experience" or "Happiness comes from within me." As you repeat this thought in your mind, continue to focus on your breath and your positive intentions behind your aspiration. You're attracting more happiness to your life with your positive energy and intentions.

When you're ready to end your meditation, let your mantra flow away and imagine that it is flowing toward the universe so that the universe may understand your intentions. Think thoughts of gratitude such as "I am grateful for all that the universe has given me." Slowly bring your focus back to only your breath. Slowly become aware of your surroundings as you drop your head forward to stretch the back of your neck, bow to the universe, and start to wiggle your toes and fingers. Then when you're ready, gently open your eyes and stretch your arms over your head.

Meditation for Weight Loss

When on a weight-loss journey, it often becomes difficult to maintain motivation and follow through with all your plans. Repeating certain affirmations or mantras during your meditative practices can help you build a healthy and happy life as well as maintain your inspiration and motivation.

Begin your meditation as laid out in the guide above and focus on your breath. As you breathe in, imagine that the air you're breathing is like a silver light that inspires you more with every breath. Feel the air as it moves to your lungs and imagine the silver rays radiating from the center of your being to the rest of your body, spreading a feeling of self-love and care. As you breathe out, imagine that the air you're exhaling is dark ash of all the negativity within you that you're expelling from your being, so that all that remains in the here and now is positivity and light. As you sit and breathe, allow the thoughts that come to mind to flow away, simply observing them without attaching any feelings to or fixating on them. As you breathe, begin to think of a mantra or affirmation with positive intentions and energy. You may want to hold the thought, "I am on this journey to become healthier and happier" or "I owe it to myself to become healthier."

When you're ready to end your meditation, let your mantra flow away and imagine that it is flowing toward the universe so that the universe may understand your intentions. Think thoughts of gratitude such as, "I am grateful for the strength and courage that the universe has gifted me." Slowly bring your focus back to only your breath. Slowly become aware of your surroundings as you drop your head forward to stretch the back of your neck, bow to the universe, and start to wiggle your toes and fingers. Then when you're ready, gently open your eyes and stretch your arms over your head.

Chapter 6: Guided Hypnosis for the Law of Attraction

A Beginner's Guide to Hypnosis

The best way to induce hypnosis is by listening to the sound of someone's voice. If you're listening to the audiobook version of this book, then you're all good to go. If you're reading this book, it would be best if you record the session or involve someone close to you to help you reach a hypnotic state. Although trained hypnotherapists are the best people to approach when wanting to reach a hypnotic state, a good friend, your partner or personally recording can help with the induction, simply by narrating the guide below.

Make sure that you clearly explain to the individual inducing your trance your intentions and goals regarding the practice. Give the individual specific phrases, affirmations, or suggestions to feed your hyperaware mind once you're in your hypnotic state. Your helper needs to be able to speak slowly and in a comforting and calming tone.

Let's begin!

Lie down on your back in a comfortable position with your hands placed on your belly, and gaze up toward the ceiling. Focus on a point in the ceiling as you become aware of your breath and gently slow it down. Breathe slowly, still focusing on that point for a few moments. Notice your eyes feeling heavier with every breath; your eyelids struggling to lift back up when you blink. Notice the sense of calm you feel when you blink; your eyelids wanting to stay closed. Your eyes are too heavy to remain open; you may allow them to gently close. Your breath is slow and steady, and your mind is calm. You're simply existing as you are. I am now going to induce the hypnotic state in which you feel happy, calm, relaxed, and at peace.

Imagine yourself in a beautiful little wooden boat floating along a crystal-clear river as you lie there. The sky is a calming blue with not a cloud to be seen, and you feel safe in the little wooden boat. You're becoming calmer and more relaxed with every breath. You can feel the warm breeze of a summer's day and the fresh smell of the grass. As you smell the air, you become more relaxed still, and you allow yourself to go deeper into your trance. It's so easy to be so relaxed, and it feels so good to go deeper and deeper into your trance. As the river flows closer to the sea, you smell the salt in the air which relaxes you more. As you relax, lying in your little wooden boat, a feeling of calm washing over you; you realize how positive, hopeful, and happy you feel. There is another gust of wind that you feel on your skin, and you go deeper into your trance. Every time you feel the wind on your skin, your trance deepens, and you feel more relaxed. You feel the boat underneath you, and you know that you're safe.

You feel happy, relaxed, and calm. You feel the wind on your skin again, allowing you to sink deeper into your trance. There is a light within you that shines on the ones that you love and brings them comfort and joy. Your inner beauty is what has allowed those around you to love you so dearly. You're a positive force of nature. Your intention is pure, and you emit positivity. The universe is working with you to help you achieve all that you want.

***

At this point in hypnosis, it is important to start feeding the person's mind with information and affirmations that will help them achieve their goals and aspirations.

Hypnosis for Love

You love yourself, and that is the most important kind of love. The love and acceptance that you have for yourself will overflow into all aspects of your life and positively influence the lives of others.

You're worthy of being loved, and the love that you're looking for is on its way to you. When you see the person that you love, you'll have the courage to do what must be done so that you may live happily.

Hypnosis for Money

The universe is sending all the wealth that you deserve your way. You're no longer scared to make difficult financial decisions. Every decision that you make will benefit you in one way or another. You're worthy of all the money that is coming your way.

You no longer need to spend money unnecessarily. You can live within your means and still save up for your future. When you spend money unnecessarily, you don't feel happy and fulfilled. Saving money makes you feel happy and fulfilled.

Hypnosis for Happiness

You're happy and relaxed. You realize that you have all the happiness you could ever need. You continue to attract happiness with your positivity and good intentions.

Happiness comes from within you. You choose to be happy by controlling how you respond in certain situations, giving you a sense of calm and peace of mind.

Hypnosis for Weight Loss

You're beautiful and kind. You'll achieve your weight-loss goals and become healthier and happier. You don't need to eat if you're not hungry.

Eating unhealthy foods makes you feel unhappy and uncomfortable. Eating healthy foods makes you feel happy and lighter. Exercising regularly makes you feel more self-confident and makes you happy.

***

You're slowly coming out of your trance. You're slowly becoming aware of your surroundings again. You can wiggle your toes and fingers and feel your body sinking into the couch. You're safe and protected. Slowly open your eyes and look straight ahead when you're ready. Blink a few times to allow your vision to adjust. Now, sit up and stretch your body, bringing full awareness to yourself.

Conclusion

"You cannot dream yourself into a character, you must hammer and forge yourself one" – James Anthony Froude (James Anthony Froude Quotes, n.d.).

With the guided meditations and hypnosis described in this book, you'll be able to bring yourself one step closer to achieving your goals and aspirations.

However, it's important to realize that meditation and hypnosis are not magical solutions to your problems. You can't meditate twice a day, every day, and then sit on the couch for the rest of the time while waiting for the universe to bring you what you desire. Unfortunately, there are no shortcuts in life. Although meditation and hypnosis do work with the law of attraction to draw your aspirations closer to you, nothing in life works unless you do!

Setting clearly defined goals and working toward these goals is a sure way to achieve them. Slap on some positive intentions, appealing to the law of attraction, and you have yourself a winning formula.

The most important aspect of using the law of attraction in life is the intention and energy behind your aspirations and your being. Positive intentions and energy are bound to attract more positivity, and the same goes for negative energy. One of your main goals in the practice of meditation and hypnosis should be to focus on positive living and intentions. In addition, practicing regular self-reflection and assessing whether your thoughts, emotions, and actions are positive or negative can give you a real starting point on what to focus on. Best of luck to you on your journey.

If you enjoyed this book in anyway, an honest review is always appreciated!

References

Ackerman, C. E. (2019, February 16). *What Is Happiness and Why Is It Important? (+ Definition in Psychology)*. PositivePsychology.com. https://positivepsychology.com/what-is-happiness/

American Society of Clinical Hypnosis. (2013). *Myths About Hypnosis*. Www.asch.net. https://www.asch.net/Public/GeneralInfoonHypnosis/MythsAboutHypnosis.aspx

Art of Living Faculty. (2020, March 17). *Alternate Nostril Breathing Benefits | Pranayama*. The Art of Living Retreat Center. https://artoflivingretreatcenter.org/blog/a-breathing-practice-to-calm-soothe-relax/

Bo Bennett Quotes. (n.d.). BrainyQuote.com. Retrieved April 29, 2021, from BrainyQuote.com Web site: https://www.brainyquote.com/quotes/bo_bennett_167549

Canfield, J. (2019, January 2). *Using the Law of Attraction for Joy, Relationships, Money & More [Guide]*. America's Leading Authority on Creating Success and Personal Fulfillment - Jack Canfield. https://www.jackcanfield.com/blog/using-the-law-of-attraction/

Cooper, B. B. (2013, August 21). *What is Meditation & How Does It Affects Our Brains? | Buffer*. Buffer Resources. https://buffer.com/resources/how-meditation-affects-your-brain/

D'Souza, R. (2019, August 29). *Affirmations*. Clinical Hypnotherapy and Stress Management Cardiff. https://www.clinicalhypnotherapy-cardiff.co.uk/affirmations/

Elliot. (2017, September 26). *The Importance of Proper Breathing for Your Overall Health | Elliot*. Elliott Physical Therapy. https://elliottphysicaltherapy.com/importance-proper-breathing-overall-health/#:~:text=The%20Breath%2FHealth%20Connection

Goodreads. (n.d.-a). *A quote from Simple Reminders*. Goodreads. https://www.goodreads.com/quotes/1307115-your-calm-mind-is-the-ultimate-weapon-against-your-challenges.

Goodreads. (n.d.-b). *A quote from The Miracle of Mindfulness*. Goodreads. https://www.goodreads.com/quotes/8207103-the-present-moment-is-the-only-time-over-which-we.

Harrold, E. (2020, October 27). *Health Benefits Of Humming & Bumble Bee Breath*. Ed Harrold. https://www.edharrold.com/post/health-benefits-of-humming-bumble-bee-breath

HMI College of Hypnotherapy. (2004, September 30). *Hypnosis - Dispelling the Top Ten Myths*. Hypnosis.edu. https://hypnosis.edu/articles/myths

https://www.facebook.com/verywell. (2019). *How Meditation Impacts Your Mind and Body*. Verywell Mind. https://www.verywellmind.com/what-is-meditation-2795927

James Anthony Froude Quotes. (n.d.). BrainyQuote.com. Retrieved April 29, 2021, from BrainyQuote.com Web site: https://www.brainyquote.com/quotes/james_anthony_froude_107683

Jewell, T. (2018). *Diaphragmatic Breathing and Its Benefits*. Healthline. https://www.healthline.com/health/diaphragmatic-breathing

Kang, S. K., Galinsky, A. D., Kray, L. J., & Shirako, A. (2015). Power Affects Performance When the Pressure Is On. *Personality and Social Psychology Bulletin*, 41(5), 726–735. https://doi.org/10.1177/0146167215577365

Kirk. (2019, April 7). *Money Meditation Techniques: Guided Meditation to Attract More Wealth*. ABUNDANATION. https://abundanation.com/money-meditation-techniques/

Learn to be calm and you will always be happy. Paramahansa Yogananda Quote. (n.d.). https://quotefancy.com/quote/884648/Paramahansa-Yogananda-Learn-to-be-calm-and-you-will-always-be-happy.

Lumen. (n.d.). *Hypnosis and Meditation | Introduction to Psychology*. Courses.lumenlearning.com. https://courses.lumenlearning.com/wmopen-psychology/chapter/other-states-of-consciousness/#:~:text=Meditation%20is%20the%20act%20of

MayoClinic. (2018). *Hypnosis - Mayo Clinic*. Mayoclinic.org; https://www.mayoclinic.org/tests-procedures/hypnosis/about/pac-20394405

Merriam-Webster. (n.d.-a). Happiness. In *Merriam-Webster.com dictionary*. Retrieved April 29, 2021, from https://www.merriam-webster.com/dictionary/happiness

Merriam-Webster. (n.d.-b). Love. In *Merriam-Webster.com dictionary*. Retrieved April 29, 2021, from https://www.merriam-webster.com/dictionary/love

Merriam-Webster. (n.d.-c). Wealth. In *Merriam-Webster.com dictionary*. Retrieved April 29, 2021, from https://www.merriam-webster.com/dictionary/wealth

Merriam-Webster. (n.d.-d). Well-being. In *Merriam-Webster.com dictionary*. Retrieved April 29, 2021, from https://www.merriam-webster.com/dictionary/well-being

Mind Tools. (2019). *Using Affirmations: – Harnessing Positive Thinking*. Mindtools.com. https://www.mindtools.com/pages/article/affirmations.htm

Mindful. (2018). *Getting Started with Mindfulness - Mindful*. Mindful. https://www.mindful.org/meditation/mindfulness-getting-started/

Peden, A. R., Rayens, M. K., Hall, L. A., & Beebe, L. H. (2001). Preventing depression in high-risk college women: a report of an 18-month follow-up. *Journal of American College Health: J of ACH*, 49(6), 299–306. https://doi.org/10.1080/07448480109596316

Ralph Waldo Emerson Quotes. (n.d.-a). BrainyQuote.com. Retrieved April 29, 2021, from BrainyQuote.com Web site: https://www.brainyquote.com/quotes/ralph_waldo_emerson_383633

Ralph Waldo Emerson Quotes. (n.d.-b). BrainyQuote.com. Retrieved April 29, 2021, from BrainyQuote.com Web site: https://www.brainyquote.com/quotes/ralph_waldo_emerson_108797

Richard Bandler. (n.d.). AZQuotes.com. Retrieved April 29, 2021, from AZQuotes.com Web site: https://www.azquotes.com/quote/703383

Schwartz, A. (2016). *The Importance of Touch - Positive Psychology*. Www.gracepointwellness.org. https://www.gracepointwellness.org/1434-positive-psychology/article/54518-the-importance-of-touch

St John, B. (2018). *Self-Hypnosis Recordings vs Live Hypnotherapy*. SelfHypnosis.com. https://www.selfhypnosis.com/recordings-vs-live-hypnotherapy/#:~:text=The%20more%20you%20experience%20self

WHO. (2019). *Frequently Asked Questions*. Who.int. https://www.who.int/about/who-we-are/frequently-asked-questions

YogicWayOfLife. (2014, April 29). *Bhramari Pranayama - The Humming Bee Breath*. Yogic Way of Life. https://www.yogicwayoflife.com/bhramari-pranayama-the-humming-bee-breath/

www.ingramcontent.com/pod-product-compliance
Lightning Source LLC
Chambersburg PA
CBHW030914080526
44589CB00010B/300